For All of My Beautiful Ghosts

Carolyn Srygley Moore

POSTHUMAN POETRY & PROSE

First published in the world by POSTHUMAN POETRY
& PROSE 2023

ISBN: 978-1-4478-2712-2

For All of My Beautiful Ghosts

Mrs Mary Frances Smith Pierce (aka mom) Painted by Mr. Crowder in 1965.

Mr Donald Brown Srygley Sr., WW2 Pacific Theatre

"Enitewok Attol, My dog, Mitzie, & pups.

I commanded harbor patrol boat during invasion."

Table of Contents

The Guest // There was no mirror

December 14, 2019

No sliver of neon plastic in which
To cohere herself.

Yet she knew. She lay like a tired dog
A large hound with soft ears
On the guest room mattress
Hair disheveled. Red bangs like lint

Gathered in her eyes the lights out only
Steam billowing from the house beyond
With snow yellow & cream
Lighting the guest room

As if it sat above a bar. She knew.
Another night. Her wrist bruised a blue
Flute yet she didn't know why.

She was too frightened to hurt
Herself. Too tired to squish a fly
Or whistle softly
Disrupt the powder
Of a winter moth's wing.

Strange. She might be happy
Inhabiting the pages of a poet
She did not know.
A voice like water & loon.

""

You are not
Spotlight eclipse
Rather, tuxedo cat familiars,
  Friend.

You are not foreign
Harvest-lined spacecraft abducting
The pale green trail
  Spark called the falling
Star.

Froth

I've shared white froth of sea
Crests shaving cream of
Home-made milkshakes
With the wrong people.
Don't trust everyone you said, I was
  Crazed with insomnia
Scratching at my face my hands.

Not betrayal.
  Indiscretions
But my best friend, old man
Without whiskey but still disorder...
  Not betrayal, that single cup of coffee
    You once purchased, for my insomnia.
Caffeine slakes the headache.

Just a blur of spirit
A black hole
A common vacuum
  Sucking cereal crumbs from a kitchen floor —
Drive the damned disorder home.

Artifacts

In a real box, teak
Inlaid
                 A graphite sketch
            Burlap blobs that seem nearly human

Or rain trickle down descendants

A rosary the girl gave
Me
            A blue arrowhead
The man of the Creek Nation left
With
The cashier; I'd served him
Eggs & orange juice
We had paused
            For victims of genocide.

An orange golf ball he passed
Over
           When he said
I had learned.

           Books.
Books from Beirut that I can read
For all ghosts

Are not the same, yet are;
Full of fingerprints
Arson
           Eradicated.

Full of the learning that stays.

Names, Sloughed

Had I not worn a nickname
To shed
   Maybe I would have molted
Too —:
Discarded my birth name,
Called myself "willow"
Or a blur of locust.

      That girl riding the carousel
   Blue frocked dress
Patent leather shoes —: four
Years old or so. Yet eyes blue & flecks
Gold at center
   Already dark circles
Vagaries of an uncertain sadness.

      My dear kid
   I will help you bury,
A pit spaded midst live wires sparking
Orange. The name we chose
For beauty
For cadence
For heritage.

         I try
To get it —: surely
You are the brave one amongst us.
Believing in the core
Self. The cat scratches the scratching
Hotel. You say you're scared
   Sometimes. A cat is omnipresent,
Omniscient,
Nearly a higher power.

         The flit & flight of you
I miss.

But bliss comes & bliss
Goes

Molts into yet another.

Strawberry wafers (displaced)

""

Relief doesn't show.
          Forecast snow crowds
Out our entries red
   Advent shutters cut into
      Calendars of joy & loss —:
   She's lost sugar cookies
Pink wafer strawberries
      Stocked in niches all over the house.

So many things to lose
Misplace
Displace

"

   Crescent moons molded
Pecan dough rolled in powdered sugar

Recipes like coffee shop receipts

A kind of cartography key // yes

Ancestry. My roots are southern
But not Confederate.

""

   But this lady is as upstate
As you can get
      Raised on talking snowmen
& the sensibility
Encouraged
   That snow people last forever

A belief clutched so

""

Even when Ben the adjacent snowball
Juggernaut
Is a puddle
  Oil rainbows
    Where the train running
Out

Leaves (she peers
Through eyelet lace curtains)

"For whom are you watching"

Imperative endings

A tall glass of iced water
    Draft as ny a cowgirl from
      A dry well
Where the rescued Iguanas fall

A walk down a corridor
   Slipped as into tunneling MRI
     Someone gentle assisting
      Elbow to bony elbow

On either saxophone side.

   It is a choice. Sometimes
  ("Take it or leave it"
But sometimes we hang on
(That scarlet leaf in the bedroom window)

(Can I tell you a secret?)
(You were my secret place)

    Morphine

A sip of it
From a cowgirl's canteen
May let her let go
  Of the ledge
    Where the kernel of wheat
  Of last dances shining
Is conceived ,
Conceives.

Perfect endings

Slipping into a wall wet yellow
The morning of rain
After dancing all night long
Slow dancing
   A bar fight in the hall

& I never knew the people of Atlantis

Wept from their pale blue gills

       Can you keep a secret?

I wish I had been there
When you slid on tap shoe
Into that wall
       That only dogs & children

See // that wall
   Of serrated orange wings.

Speaks of sails, of red sailboats launching

Speaks of sails,   of red sailboats launching
    & I remember your hands

Guiding.   From across many
Rooms.   You had power, know it,   knew
It.   But you never touched

Me,   except to pass a pen a book a piece

       Of unsigned paper.

You could have hurt me, but good man, dear

Face of molting masks
Of temperance &

       No pseudonyms, trespass
In that way

That way
You never did. Lighthouse man
Spinning light
Like yarns
No.

       Hurt me, you never did.

Mimes

That man shuffling to Smokey
  On the yellow dirt curb
    That night I was leaving.
Packing Rimbaud Nietzsche Wilde
  Boxes damp from yesterday's
    Thunder, a little bit scared
I smoked a cigarette torn of filter
  Fingertips stained yellow
As from daffodil dust, a little bit
  Scared. You had said
    That I was the one
Who made you hit me
  & it wasn't bad, could've been so
      Bad. The iron
Of that porch rail struck struck
  But I made you do
It, you said, said you spent
The night
      After I ran
        Bashing your face into
Mirrors, prints R brought here
  From Jamaica. Seems that,
    Everyone does it,
Blames & shames
  & as I was leaving sweet Smokey
    Shuffled a tune or two,
Then he went singer to singer, song to song
  Landed like a
Mime —: drops pounding
  A student ghetto awning —: *I had never seen such rain.*

As Moons Root

   middle of a rounded room
packing boxes & totes piled with goth
Plot & resin chipped ravens
   Black roses root, as moons root.

The collar belonging to a red hound
Now homed in the yard
       A plot of land ten foot square.

We spade unthinking midst live wires...
       they closed the pit
   As God of all genres might shut

A portal . The gravedigger said
Cover; coyote & red fox called, he said,
Summoned
    To the smell of corpse .

A new ending; there was no stench.

In aorta I sit shiva,
Rife tides of treason
    As the blood rain falls.

A God's Prayer —

The many versions a child takes...

What is it
To reject your child, living breath
Calling out from the blue porch steps
   Momma
     Daddy
Where the cat hid to hatch her kittens.
What is it like
     To call out the urchins
        Contours blurred
Of our shared histories, to call them out
Into the village square for shaming. Quiet
  Stoning via any means
        Cut a lock of hair
Yellow
    Place in an envelope
& mail it to whatever god is in your prayer.

Desert Affirmations //

The Black Tambourine shifts on
A moonlit dresser & I see Mazzy Star
Eyes shut moving within
            shining octaves.
These are savage, capricious
    Lawrence of Arabian

Deserts. Open the skull
With hatchets there is blood.
Open the cactus, water. Sweetheart
        As you woke from that self
Induced coma

I found a way to figure it out
There are ways to figure it out…who is
            the soldier?
Or, on a different sheet of paper, how does
    the moonlight

Traipse the player piano keys
    Like a grieving mother
Elephant // how
Their ghosts appear like yellow plumed fog
Flailing a bit
        As if to confirm what matters.

The Old Days // Thanksgiving

Call em
War stories — awkwardly
    Zigzag

Orpheus sought sobriety & opium
      Little exits
& calling card
  Invitations
To enter novellas scribed
    By candle
Under// within
Hollows...Brontë sisters

We had similar characters
  Heathcliff
    Eyre, cries from moor & tower

(
What is pause
What is silence)

Phoenix & acetaminophen
  in theory
Least
Gather the water falling aorta
cupped hands (& what is
  A leaf?)

Bashing origin
Bashing the cradle.

Moats

He held me down — not in a bad way —
    Our bodies etched in sand
        Castle constructs
(What is the kiss
But a troubadour roar) dusk tides &

        Stars fell in my opening mouth
   My opening
Youth
So sudden I nearly choked
On the pitch dark
Shine
The black obsidian.

Along this trail trod gravel

Along this trail trod gravel
& rising myrrh

    Omniscient
  Wise kings
We leash our ghosts.

  orange tether
The tone of a golf ball a man named
Viktor once gave
   Like iced water in a blue glass

When he said that I had won.

Desk stocked with hollows
  Where
Ghosts left notes for preceding
Centuries—; the 3 cats, gone now.
Grinning like little pitbulls.

& Melville linked blue paw round

      absence.
That day he was shadow along
Scissored glints a red bowl
Giant soul
   drinking water I knew old man you —

      His blinded eyes
Veered.

      The shine the shine
  Was his own.
He gave me a cube of it
Dissolved with
A wheelbarrow of lemons
  In a patio iced tea

I won briefly Viktor.
Disorder crept back in.

Combat colonization

Eye white to eye white
Yet — no excuses.

      There are the victims.
They were only carrying trains full
Of flowers.

""

There are also victors, yes //
   The man knew to combat, eye white to eye white
& sprang. Heroes breathe life
Into tree limbs, force past

      Taking the thing down...

""

  "Thing.." objectification.
We are all trees.

""

Unfortunately, monstrosity
Often exhibits human
     Hands, this superlative
        opposable thumb.
What I would trade sometimes,   to be   myth
Of great beast,   termed sweet
Mountain
    Gorilla eventually.

""

Or Frankenstein's creature
Before hurt & ridicule
Changed him,

       Tore at the visage that when sleeping
Was lovely,   calm with lofty
      Not yet inaccessible.

Dolphins Liminal

The depth of blue, it is
    unfathomable
As depth of sea. Before radar

The dolphin let the
Lost sailors in. Maybe if that interval

(Spent ghostlike between two lives
A canal connecting
Hemispheres.)

    Hadn't occurred
The constant hum you make when
You touch

    My face, as if I am a cradle ,
Would remove the detail

Of every second
    Every goddamn second.

But Fire.   We are combustible

Still just kids, nearly similar

But not alike
Alike
At all

    Except for

    Depth, that Blue deepening
At the core where is —
      Some facts of what water means

As the dolphins call.

Watercolor.

Zigs of pale stone,   Pink
In a way the world never is. Landscapes —

Silences, ridiculous endings.
Smoke rising indigenous, peace
Or fission. Globs or strands...

Sandbars.

Where he stranded you, that paper
Ship that could have been
An airplane also. It returned

Not the same
People,   a different dialogue.
A sensibility.   The sky mirrors no face
But the lucent haze

A good swim might leave
On the river between us.   A little
Bit purple, as veins may be.
I'm sick of anger

When a few words would clear things,
Misunderstandings
    Spinning on the crib
Like a juggernaut world globe.

Cant look too close.
Its terrifying
      As the thought of jumping
    When its only water
& you know very well how to swim.

The disturbance

When I visit
   It's like you've been Aslan in
A globe of blasted. Sand
   What is glass formed of

When I visit
   Its like I've never
Stepped into the role
   Of activated marionette.

Sand blasted. & what are pieces
Of shattered glass?
Where is the sandcastle
   Where is the first dew of sand?

Nonsense is everything.
I was a message in a tin can
   A note scrawled to some
Kid

& there went time.
There went time

   Maybe
I messed up
But I always messed
Up
      Trying.

Fire & glass.

Once I asked why he always gives DVDs

Once I asked why he always gives DVDs
You said
Don't you know why
Its because that's his only way to tell us he loves us

—

//

What is this shining boundary

What is this shining boundary
The capsule rocket the kitchen roach
This glitter of puddling sun-water

What is this sweet artistry
This sweat pooling rosa & sage
To guard our compass.

The days of calling: the name
That molts & molts but does not leave

What are these syllables dragging
Suture gut torn with the teeth.

What are these flights from the ordinary?
The ones with hollow broken teeth
The ones that gnaw.

The world is raw as just slaughtered lamb.
The one who raised it
Called it by a child's name; yet when
Slaughter came,
Nobody said a prayer.

Then
The air was full of moths, shuffling
Like little white whispers.
Somebody nibbled the air.

Don't tell him, it's his last octave.

    Perhaps, perhaps
He knows —:
   It's the glitter of it
Just a mercurial bully
      Outer space shapeshifter
Trying to root like yellow
Forsythia costumed
Hemlock.

Freedom in the Gulag

In that place
Of criminal carousel
Mimicry

     He talked of selling weed.
  His swollen face
Resigned.

I said if I was a street singer
I'd free a gulag monkey from its parrot
Cage & teach her to fret guitar
With me // mend the strings

   Snapping like bazooka.
He said if he was a medicine man
He would not neglect
The body, but be careful
As he with wounded orchids
Tended the mind.

/// November 28 2022

Bury a leaf with a pebble
By a river
    For Adam & Howard the beagle

RIP //

Rummy

He tossed the deck of playing cards
   Each turned to a bird
Not dove nor vulture

     But hummingbirds suckling
Our hearts our mouths. Hungry
  So hungry

Eat & nibble the seed
& fly whirring as sharks move
    Graceful souls shimmying

  Simply to stay alive.

Peach Stones, whistler

Its a brief space, this place
Of broken tree limbs & ghost stumps.
   The numb arm thunks
Against the wall
When he moves.
      Catches on the edge
Of wire shopping carts,   stone
Cats,   anything
   To be kept.
Everything is vulnerable, someone
Once muttered his way, like
   A suitcase voice. The salesman
In the playwright brain
Flutters in his grey suit a bit
   Flaps, a bluefish on a landing,
Then passes as the drawbridge
Opens, a pinch of scale
     A ridge of gill
Floating, drifting
   Anonymously
     As a peach stone buried.

Is there water?

After it all
   They hush me, calm down
Down. The baby doll was never set
On fire.
After it all
I ask
Is there at least a pool of
Water
    If not fresh
Then stale from a suburban pond?

Bury me with a pebble
In my fist
    A rose petal between my lips.

     Yes
They say
   There is water there. The ice chip
   Pail
Received once the gut stitch
Cut
   Recedes.

""

The halo's bark blocks the call of
The
Loon.
""

Let us not talk about brevity.
Why should we be marred by brevity.
""

Never wanted to
Be a princess

    In those off shoulder gowns
Lack & lace
Emphasized

A sandwich bag of
Yellow
Pills
Bumblebee
Black beauties.
""

& in the car
The so macho Diva
Barked with his radio
Handle
    A wench for a nickel //

Market place ripoff.
""

He said: can it pull a cart.
They said: you mean she?

I am the shoddy white wooden cart
In a wink full of flashes,
The hare & the man & the palm.

What is a leaf?

""

The Crane Whoops

The white & black crane whoops
   & somewhere in the orient
Mates
Dances with another
Creature
    & I

Appreciate who we are
Despite it all

As the lake loon calls.

The purpose of trinkets

They pin the fog down.
   Like sumo wrestlers
      Like colonialist
  Dung beetles
Pushing the sun...

Elephant snow globes, hollowed skull
& rosé bottle paperweights.
Little souvenirs from roadside stands,
   hex signs, fireworks.

Wrestlers —: pin the loss down.
""

   Nothing diminutive about birthdays...
""

   I saw a man — a guess —: think skin Walker
Or Big Foot,
Confident stride through traffic
Like a man
    Confiscated, gutted
  Walking into a corridor of stations
Of motionless freight
Trains.

     Some
Movie stars threw salt packs //
Brown lunch bags of peaches
   Caught by a hunger

Where the wall
Ended
& portal trees
  began.

INTERLUDE X X

noun
plural noun: ghosts
1. an apparition of a dead person which is believed to appear or become manifest to the living, typically as a nebulous image."the building is haunted by the ghost of a monk"
""

Similar — //

specterphantomwraithspirit
soulshadow
presencevisionapparitionhallucinationbodachDoppelgängerduppyspoo
kphantasmshaderevenantvisitant
wight eidolonmaneslemures // excerpts, Oxford Thesaurus //

Its all astronomy to me

Its just astronomical, mechanics
Of vehicle
Corridor clocks.

& I consult
Howard,   a beagle, a muncher
Of carrots   leader of kayaks
Green with summer
          For he has taken care
Of that human, ten years now

    When questions
Of hybrid sunlight or moonlight or
    Why
Is the sun right
There & so
Scarlet

I ask a mechanic of snowplow
Engines mechanic of
    Temperance

          Who asks Howard the tricolor
Hound.
    Howard sings. Pitches his head
Back casts his bay to a roar
          Keeping predator
Grief away.
                What, when they who
Guard us
From abyss
They who keep us to the lake
Edge
          Where ice crack webbing out
From center
          Need our turn

    Carrying down
Down

    Into the nebula
Where is
The dog doppelgänger
I call out Howard like a book character
    What is the mission
But a new astronomy
A new astronomer

       & some rest
Some rest
For
       The beagle round the leader
Of kayaks green with summer
The fact of who
     Extinguishes the effigy grotesque
Leads us
Leaves us
Something of solidarity

      A man & his dog
A boy & his dog
Digging for the fossils
The fossils we will be.

For Howard. RIP d., 11/28/22.
One of the coolest dogs I've ever known.

Eating Swans over the Hudson

Swan weathervanes, spinning

The week in the news

In a room
  of blue thresholds & bright
Crosswalks,   a man began
Constructing walls made
Of flowers.   Each wall signed
By an anonymous
    Being
      Who stumbles error to error.
   Words taped to his
Body flailed in disorder.
He was obsessed by taking
All that scared him, all
That to him was unknown,
& taping
    It down in some order. He thought
      There are means by which
    Chaos can be refuted. Obsessed.
""

But all the birds!! All the flowers!!
Trains crushed deer in the crosswalk.
Corridors where mothers
Nursed &. burped infants peacefully suddenly
    flooded,
    condemned.
""

    // Integration of disorder
        With wound & mango //
     Said Rimbaud
As Gauguin went the river
      South. Nothing to do //

2.

Nuclear towers shrieked alarms, leaked, threatened
meltdown
Workers zipped in orange
Jumpsuits run!
        Run against locked walls.
        Disposable.

        "

// Do we stay
Do we leave // to unlearn
To unremember? All the kids
        Swimming — skipping school
— dead by cancer
Within 45 years. Visited by
Mephistopheles.

        "

Like a leaf cupped
Like dew vintage sipped
We are what's floating
In the middle. Wound //
Vietnam

Walls of fallen

        & failed
Ideals turn

Cannibal.   Maybe
There's no way other than
Home. Maybe it is another piracy
Another lynching // piggy's head :
        Maybe

        "

        Dry
Vines
Dense in trenches

Combat
Cesaire & his lovers & revolution

Begin feeding greedily
        Flowers choking the threshold
                The crosswalks
            & dying off a little
One by one
Like wide doll eyes.

 Eventually Cesaire poses:
" eat. —

So the passages
Can be trespassed
Transgressed
        Open passages & pastures, outer
            Be perceived. // Realizing
            What
Is
Happening."...

""

Supermarket candy foil rattling linoleum
Empty spaces
Scattered singing
    Twitching on baking aisles
Gasp gasp
You know asthma can kill
            You know, in New York
            They've begun dining
Upon the once spared bird
Elegiac
For
Grace.
        Stable, reassuring elemental
            Beauty.

"

Swan blood red. Swan
Is like chicken,
Boiled crow, broth
Red
Violet
Mauve
          A vulnerable
Ideal
   As mountains crashed by Ra.

For my beautiful 29th Street

Like a kid straddling a cirrus cloud
Pretending I was a player
Of men or angels...a harpist

Next row house down 29th stepped
Out from his window
Played water from strings
Pulled language // curatorial
discovery

& I read the Notebooks of Malte
"Such Things" he calls
Them, these cuneiform marked lice
Combs

More beautiful
For being a part of daily
Routine. Rituals are the hush the noise
Watermark

A spoon rattling
A coffee cup or the lipped
Cereal bowl or going for a swim, three
Pm, sudden bells of rain.

Not the Opera's phantom

(The ghost of blame)

   Phantoms
surround demand: surrender.
I have
Nibbled daisies for them, retched
As if the
Nub was peyote // some soul
   Purgation

""

Anxiety spinning
      wheel spokes,
Hubs. Never had A hallucination
Except for my ribs that day.   Tremor
Sketched in blurred charcoal
   Over the bathroom mirror
      In fog
Ribs coming undone

""

The water is clean enough.
The waste boiled away.

""

Even dirty
 Weeds, pulled from the anorexic
Garden, can be boiled
Even fried-up with onions
     Setting the curtain
   Daffodils
On fire.

""

Yesterday driving fairground avenue
   An older woman watched

One
Falling star
     Green & rife with sparks
& a memory
Of not leaving,
Not walking.
       Feeding
The wound that is blame
  Nurtures
    The liar eye.

The purpose of Memorials

(Sandyhook, December 14, 2012)

      Perhaps
I guess
   Memorials
Must do sometimes

We've been
To Newtown
   Driven down
Driven past the razed orchard.
   Bought summer
Peaches at a small market.
Bitten
  Into flushes
    Of sweet.

      Will you sit with
Me
Father of Daniel
Fathers & mothers
    Lay wreathes in the circling
Current
Watch the flowers bear
Your grief
   Away.

      Kissed toads upon
Lily pads.

Circles of cut stone.
Great runes of Sandyhook
   Are you too
The sundial
Star dial
      Paper reams of first
    Four leaf clovers

Falling
Flash
     Perhaps a satellite
Naive & shining an elliptical
  Of souls.

Maybe adults know a different kind of God.
   Eddying
     Faces marked
By the great sycamore hybrid at center
A child's face
   Elementary
In each & every leaf.

Parachutes full of Dogs

Sky.   Wrapped like wood grain
Like tortilla
Like saying hello in a different country.
Sky.

Brain injuries can be favorable—:

A new mode of speech
A word string, cut

Threads. Approach me with
Machete scalpel kitchen scissors.
   I see the space between
Myself & thought.

That night approaches
My arm flailed my future dropped
Like a lozenge
Into a bastard mouth

Sky. I love it anyway.
Nice here. Parachutes full of dogs.
All forms of resistance.

Only a feather displaced.
The falconer yellow lure
The ball bobbing
    Blue fishing hook toy.

Even when it came at me

Even when it came at me
Elbow crooked
As if raising a white umbrella
As if to strike a mirror

  I knew
Everyone has more than one reflection.
I went upon the mirage
watering hole

     I knew it was valid
For all the elephants
All the lionesses
Gathered to drink

In unison…
Even when it tried to get me;
What I remembered myself to be;
I had something left

I had you,
I had water too. Cold, real
The stuff of sleepy New York cowboys.

What's chasing me now;

        not that
Juggernaut of refugees
Crying out
Better home than here.

   ◦ not that 3 piece suit man checking the bus schedule
   ◦ As I stood stranded
   ◦ Not that man
   ◦ On top of me until he realized
   ◦ I was the stronger.

The storm roots deep.
& if I had no voice
Of screams?
      I thrash I thrash pink-flowered
(i remember exactly)
    Panties torn
At the ankle

I got free.   Migratory,
free

Hauntings

Hauntings
   Gathered from the rough
      The Susquehanna

Always looking for a river
A bend circling
Bundles of extra clothing simple rags by which to cover
  Essentials

Love. The sandwich was bad today,
Bread soggy
Turkey ripe.

I focus on the bend,
Hope I'm not the only one seeking to ease
Your face-off
  confronted, intersection of indecency
& a wall of   instant mortality

I swear
You'd think it was oatmeal, institutional potatoes,
How immune we become.
  These slaughters by fate.

Hauntings, hands

Hauntings
Hands
   & Dumpy Motel Rooms

Our hands with their marvelous
Sandwich & red plum bearing
    Thumbs

Are much of us. What else do we have
    Really. The grit of it.

""

Here we arrive
These Vermont hotel rooms
With promising water;
   "What a dump" I say;
"That much the better" you say.
Drunk with escape we laugh

""

   Evergreens. Fractious
Boulders that are my pillow.
My pulse.

       Hands.

""

    Factories
Along the backwoods path
" It's so dark" I say
" that much the better" you say —:
   Your hands. Your thumb at base
Rounded perfectly—-

""

  Bone. Malleable
Or axe taken to skull, yet

Erodes
    Elemental as shoreline.

Waiting canyons, streaked scarlet
Lavender
    Petals bled gentle
       This mountain stone.

I will always remember you.

The construction workers

The construction workers dismantle
The cards the glass the pebbles
&
Bits of stone.
    I don't know any more
What windows
Are made of. The breadcrumbs
    Of doorways.
  The spinning feathers are infallible.
& I ask
Them,
                Pink pink
       House of plastic
Flapping at hourglass apertures

Give me a flask.
    Tell me of windows.
  I will nibble crumbs
As deer gnaw at bright bright daffodil.
& I will disappear

In an oasis of reinvention
I will appear.
    Chaos defeated, emerge.
        Reappear.

Conversation with my own ghost

Coming up the gravel path a mountain
Mauve with West Virginia time
Elapsing in a manner
Defiant of clockwork cog
& nerve. We didn't speak a word.

Later, when the hotel electric lanterns
Clicked off come dusk
& bedtime I told you of that boy
I loved: he came to me
Hanging from the step of a paused

Train waved then drifted away
Along crests of rain & slashing
Light ephemeral to the eyes.
We didn't speak a word. A red
Bird clung to a pitted moon .

There was no necessary word.

Splash of Paint

Rained today
A splash of paint thrown into
A peeking light
   Nearly eclipsed.

Sun changed its mind
Whimsical
As the eighteenth century
   Gemini.

That was some years ago.
A different machine..

Walking 29th in Baltimore
By a canal
Where a body
    discovered itself

Like a famished bone slug
Feasting upon a pebble.

On the leaf
Edge where
   Dust wings reign -/; glistening

A kind of
    Hollywood.

      The body rested in the night song of
        Conch.

""

Indigo
   spectral space, color

    Obliterated
   Like that planet we
Learned to be history. Prehistory

—a boat unmoored —
　　In shadow drifts. The ebb
The flow

Cheers

Our diner
You had red curly hair the uncommon
   Kind genetic not bottled
You kicked me under Formica
Burnt with cigarettes maybe
   A cigar tip or two.

Our diner
We talked Matisse work in blindness
   How Borges laugh
Was fat & filled the room
A student asked how he selected motel
   Room numbers
For a story I cannot recall.

      Horizons
         Layered like sunflowers &
Sub flooring
Tawdry & beautiful
Sat like an archaeologist's
Excavated
   Bones & arrows & effectual
Goodness.

   Cheers.

Of Feral Angels

you're doing OK. integrity is something

        Where's home
   Said the snowman
Tapping his cigarette.

The feral angels called as the barn owl called
   Round faced as a spinning world
     Globe.

Can't stop crying she says. not wet faced
but wiping mud of crematoria ash from my loves
The room isn't dark
   Enough

I can still see. I hear you
He says
    Thoughts of a girl on a train

Gathering grins into a lace
Handkerchief
   Handing them
Out

   With fresh bread
     Some tea & patio lemons sliced in giant yellow
first invented
wheels

junkyards of love & desire

Daedalus flight &   chess of
   Falling.

Cutting Scales from Sailfish

you saw it before I did

That floundering

a serrated blade

glass / grass — a

bird

A feather white

Frail

A sailfish scale frail

As surrender

Mirror / pasture

manifest

aid of torn waking

Whistles

Kettle & fear..

I know now

You don't believe me

Not even

That pact ghosts whisper & slice

Spit & blood.

When the Train Passes & I Can't See you any more

Most difficult things
About waiting

Snow days

Counting seconds between

Each webbed parachute white

Feather

Or sweating drip drip in interrogation chairs

The chandelier bears the crosshairs

Of a sniper decision.

Its a marathon of crime dramas

No buses are running

Train leaves traces of smoke

& dust along the trajectory of

Failed loves

// who are you living
For //

Saving lives of boys & dogs

Unemployment

(We've had this conversation
Where I see birds
You see trees)
"

    That morning
Troy held us
In its hollow

     & I was late
For a temp interview // when I know
Myself to be
An impostor

    Anxiety is everything
Is imbuing
       Blood waterfalls

   Unemployed
Looking into the shallows
A tin of mustard herring. I was late

Full of bus station clatter
Old women speaking forecast
In the background
      & talk of Genet
    Stealing bread
So he could write flower ladies
Locked in prison.

Unemployment sucks.
Ah I'll put on my cream gown
I'll look like my mother
// she never got fat //
    & we will rest in the hollow
Fetal sac
Philosopher Plato

Leaning back
   Sucking our fetal hands

Soul mates
   Anger
Tins of ravioli, at last something

   Feeding the little
Kids.

As someone once told me,

As someone once told me
Hell is here on earth. damn But the snow is glorious. Screw it
Get out the blue saxophone.
Bite down on the reed. Spit a little. Play

I didn't get it

    O baby R

That hurt how you hurt

We invaded Iraq

    Your brother Billy
     Came to you
Walking out from the pond where only death treads water

Lily pad lily

        You drove down coast
Past eunuch castles (Candide//
Candide)
    Paces pacing
Your long black raincoat from the surplus store

Black glasses swallowed
Hallucinations

Baby R baby

     You'd gone to the base
   Where Billy's camp occurred
Before Nam took him
Husked him
Flew him home ready for shooting up

    That's one transition
Soldiers choose
I suppose

Baby R baby

     I'm sorry I could not see
   The big brother you cradled
Buried honorably in the scepter Gettysburg graveyard

Grinding a cigarette butt
Out / out
At the marker

little white crosses // inked black
x on the eye-doll

Wand.

Will you still like me // the Circadian Spirit

"

If you know I never wear a dress
Without paisley leggings
    60s pink & blue

If you know I carry pigeon feathers
In my wallet
    The green feathers
        From the breast

If you know my father was nicer
   After duel-noon rose
     & the vodka ice clanked
     & the transparent curse ended //

Circadian
   The cadence //

      Ice trays
    Are slim or meant for seas
& as my blood sugar falls off a cliff
  & I get bitchy

    Hey
Will you still like me
If you know I need a wedge of
Chocolate stuffed with almonds
   To be consistent

    To be more than simply
Ephemeral & mercurial
   & usually
     kind.

Liberation // anniversary 46

For Sally W & her Babushka

Portrait:

  A circle barbed wire
    Knotted threads throughout

I see a woman.
   A rib of a person.
She is smiling. Oval brown eyes —
The color of evergreen bark —
Squinting into the fog.
   She is putting a step
Into composure,
Even
   Beauty
Forward; as women are taught
To do.

    A man salutes alongside her;
As if holding a bowler hat
Over his heart.
  He thinks of pianos, looks vaguely
At they who are eating sandwiches
Salami & cheese, cruelly
Thoughtlessly.

When I was 15, a girl called Sally
Whose Babushka passed vaguely
   The fog the black fog
In Auschwitz's chimney stacks
   The diaspora
Of gene & fingerprint

Told me I could never
Truly truly understand.

& in that Moment, the expression
On her face, her so personal
	Yet inclusive
Embrace of truth & tragedy
Now ring generous & true.
""""

"listen to every word."

46th anniversary theme.

Six million Jews
& millions of "Others" targeted
Were slaughtered by
The Reich's
So-called "final solution".

Waterhole spirit

Blood on
Ivory
Piano keys

Where she drew forth pails of water
Streams of river
Chopin & Brahms.

      Crickets by the creek guiding the octaves
   Joined in; children
      On treehouse floors
Turned to the ephemeral

   Red, red.

      Blood on piano keys —:
  Surely
The mama elephant wailing I hear
      Piercing grief
Over the baby
   Slaughtered
But barbarians exist everywhere
  & the poached gutted face
Of family
Mama papa o baby baby

I am seeking the waterhole
That is no mirage
   A washcloth
A rag
By which to wipe the keys.

The Insomniac's Redemption (of men & doves)

For Donald Brown Srygley Sr., my father.

Walking the bend
Walking the downpour
    A stunned dove plunked before us.
       You dried her wings & eyes
With the soft
Lining of your green jacket.
She looked at you for a moment
   A gaze neither lopsided
Nor cross eyed,
& in the jazz club finger snap
As blue ran rampant
     She appeared to die.

You know
I've seen men die a zillion times
  Or was it twice? —
Wrapped lovers in soft white camisoles
Prayed wildly to the humpback
   Clouds, placed heirloom hand
Mirrors before
Their mouths & seen no breath.
    I've stopped clock & watch

When heart
When brain
Forfeited promise & accountability...

Next morning
The dove wound like
A top
   Twirled thrice a napping dog
Then tossed the earth away.
& the men, each
A semblance of my father
     I found rowing away

From the aircraft carrier
Having killed
In the Pacific
    Having been killed in the
Theatre
        & managed to move away.

Just last evening
Half past sundown
    I understood
The clocks came out of hiding.
I kissed them, each.
Breathed deep.
    Slept well, first time in a while.

Bicycling Backward

For George

    Going backward
Bicycling
I feel wind cupping my back
My pelvis

I feel nothing.

""

I've told my life to sceptics.
    Bicycling backward
Branches lashing my faces
Layers of faces

I felt nothing.

""

Maybe I'm looking for Jesus
    Some mentoring soul
  A bird a dog a man perhaps

So the holy water will not scorch
& sizzle

My esophagus
As it drains down.

""

I'm telling my life to a sceptic.
    He snuffles a bit like a hound
Tracing
Seeking out
Landmine & snuffles a bit.

Focus he says focus.

""

I've smeared gasoline over the lens.

& the fright-match of arson
Is at hand.

I see face on face
A barmaid insomniac trying to sleep.

Fright match of arson at hand.

Safe & Sacred Places

Safe & Sacred Places // essential;
     Endangered.
"

"Severe weather alert
Xy county."
"

The alert
Husk-radio cabinets exist no more
These houses that exist
     Only to be remembered.
Mom would talk a little
About the mahogany cabinet
     That resounded.
Pearl Harbor
War of the Worlds—:

Drove yesterday along Goode Street.
The hospital on the left
A small iron wrought chair
Planted
     For someone who passed —:
Cancer. Good people, a veterinarian //
Of capability
A cadenced love of garden
Passes through my aorta
     Waterfall skinny dipping
       As in the wake
         Moccasins circled

Like a dream of water
A dream of piss
A dream of blood monsters
     Drunk with poppies & milk

Fresh from momma cows
Calves torn away

Milked grief

& into my truth I doze
We are here for the cows
Horses the dogs
The owls
We are here for each-other.

"

& here
The farm houses
Constructed around bomb shelter
Domes // cellars
That have no stairways
Beyond stakes
The hunter drives down deep
Into the dove coo
That seeks me out.

"

Coming toward me
Walking against the rivulet
Salt-stung passenger cars

A couple & a yellow dog.
The man waves gently
Without wince
Upstate New York strangers

Simply
Knowing I too I tend.

Although truly
I never
In early youth
As the iris bulbs buried
As tomato plants burgeoning

Were stripped bare
    Petal & fruit —// never
Paid much attention to the gardener
    pianist fingers
        drawn rivers of Chopin

Rather the dogs
The cats
    The tangerine canary singing
In bursts from a levitating cage

      near
A safe place
    Sacred as lullaby invented
Rooted deep in my DNA.

Hummed nightly
Chords
Words
      Never written down.

Fry me up an egg Bubba

This
Global
Heat
Indifferent as was his belly

    God or that massive trucker

That axial weight
Paralyzing.

""

Only
    I seek
An anodyne
For matted nets
Chaos

    The tangled mess still
   Trapped
In pond ice.

""

A remedy
For that conversation
   With spearmint tea on a patio

   Urns spilled
Smitten
By ash

""

& by
Speech
You granted me
Name

Though I already had
Existence.

""

We come
From different
Houses

Inclinations
Different
Pots & pans & what
Our skillet

Is used for.
Fry me up an egg Bubba
""

Red maps
Train rails sketched white

Infrastructure
Buckling

As butterflies too melt.
    Can the monarch secrete
  Its poison?

Licked wings
Rendered salvageable after all.
""

You may hold me down
Pin me to cork like dawn
  I'm ok with the written wall

      Heat

Brings out the beast in me.
Hirsute as a being

Only electromagnetically
Acknowledged

  At one point
The unwritten wall.

""

The well
That has consumed

    Pterodactyl
& white rhinoceros

Is, still

  A gutted earth
A gutting yawn

What happened to Orpheus —

Rebuilding the geode
That rock split open like a raven egg
  Hatching
These sparkling mini cliffs & caves.

Rebuilding the box
Krapp"s last tape
Last cigarette
Last rainbow banana

  I saw Harry Smith
Caught in a trash can
     Like a fish in a dry well
  Ringed
Echo

      Homeless
    Climbing out of the doubt
The Baltic error
The drought.

He climbed out
Of our kiss
    Kicking out stairs

From that hourglass pillar of salt... seems

Nobody looks behind
Them any more
Lot's wife
   & Eurydice
Fairly lost
Fairly left with the dry well trout
Behind.

Yes

I've written it in blue ink
On masking tape pieces
Torn from the wheel

I've written it, newspaper block
Print, mailed
To some PO BOX

I've written it, permanent black mark
Over my mouth
The apex of
My wishes

      Today I ignored
Hexagonal stop signs
Prefabricated for the sticks

        Some kind of absurd
Pluto erased
Discarded

  Resuscitated

  Yes
Yes.

Hanging Out

We loiter at a service station. Could
Be a castle, ice & sand. Gertrude
Is nibbling a chocolate bar, wobbling
Like a toy on bionic hips. We loiter.
From some car radio a country song
Regarding Jesus & second chances.
You might need that Gertrude said
A few years back; I don't. Her hands
Twitched. We loiter.

I'm eating sugar crusted peach
Gummies. The service station, like
A warehouse laundromat, has black
Hole windows. The OPEN sign still
Blinks. Winks. Around it, gas pumps
Were exhumed or laid to rest. Like
Ukraine I say. What drops
The bomb? Castles melt or get stomped
Upon; tides swoop turquoise rings
Collected over lifetimes; diamonds
Pop from Art Deco wedding rings.
Gertrude says something about Mary
Shelley, the first true feminist. Read
Frankenstein, she whispers . Only
Then will you understand.

Untitled

Man
I miss you
    That electric shag carpet
    The trailer of many rooms.

I miss all of you. A society
  Of sorts
The student ghetto
      A commune

Kneeling in banked dirty snow
Planting broccoli &
    Digging up that hemlock
Grown
For cats. O Baltimore down
      To
The cinema past nudes painting
Nudes in ice frosted windows

It's just chocolate fudge swirl, loss

Some feed
It by ciphering memory
    Hey, if I
Ignore it
          I am
That thing
I chose
        To not become—: never
Posed nude but once

    To have shelter
    She tiptoed a daylight massage

& saw
& was
        Like a saleswoman
Traveling saw

The worst
In men
    In women.

If you can remember the smell of
Just washed baby pajamas
Or the spill off hash smoke under glass
Or fireflies diffracted in the harbor

You're probably going to be fine.

SLOTHS

The world is terrifying
Guess what
We are the world only a little
Pebble & grit
Light & salt correcting the blueberry stain
    On my white bell sleeve

   There's no point to oven it
  Children waiting for breakfast
In the next room well everyone knows that one...
      Festivals sour.
Terrifying. Apples stocked are soft
   Says T
Add butter I say fry em up I say

     My niece draws a picture of a sloth
   For my birthday
& of course I tell her --: even T S said poets are necessarily
Lazy
       When she calls the lights
Are out
  I am sleepy
Always sleepy
    Never really truly
  Sleeping

My best friend once woke on the other side
Of a ledge
      Skipping rope
Chanting
   Happy as a train wreck. Is what is.

If I touch
The world
      I will unruly scream. Die

Sleeping
Scream.

August Rituals

We park the slate car
    By a hill of just harvested peaches. Tomatoes
        Round as halos
Pile in an old brown lunch bag...

    Could've been anyone

I guess? No
Not really
   But the homeless have laughed
& wept in the dark recesses
   Crazy
Of sex & fury.
""

      You aren't homeless
Any more but remembering
    We were, all of us were
       Underwater
Breathing
Where nobody thought such things possible. Possibility
  & hey probability

     isn't just a secular green
Pool table
   Cue to the ball.
""

     You start dipping naan rounds
In garlic hummus
        But it's not that easy

I say
      Biting the round.
Or is it? Couldn't have been just anybody I say.

Not that.

""

Tonight I will color my hair
The soft yellow of lanterns
As if I am a window

I will figure out Kafka
& Solzhenitsyn
As the trains call at 3 am.

& we
Will pause
    Alight darkness
  Selves carry

Like a red suitcase of hammers taking
      It
            On.

Quiet August Snow

Resistance parachutes rippling violet
    Always
A shade of red

      A cat flashes yellow teeth in a tree somewhere

A man stands atop a gutted nuclear reactor

  A few men, disowned

Perhaps

      A pit bull cries out--:

& last dusk light I went off on him a bit

Colonialism is never ok
   & what is war crime
      What is genocide

At the end of a day
As journalists say
     Bones ground to fleck

   Parachutes succeed
Parachutes fail

      Names & nations slough away

& love's skin thins
    Tearing as lovers age

         Apple core white as camisole

     Seeds dark the fugitive cyanide

& old cultures stand strong.
    Violets grace the vinegar tumbler

      As all returns origin
     Radioactive slime & people

Out
Of

Water.

The Painter & the Photographer

For Georgia O'Keefe

Keep telling Stop there's a light
   Up there, across --
Below. The rain crazed her that after-
      Sheen
     & the memory, the northeastern
Trees opening wide
Like flowers
   Or bison skulls ferrous red
Mid a painter's desert
       Migrating
     As a photographer
    Set to high Def
& photographed her in the rain
  That tollbooth keeper laughing
     Toothless
   At bends in the desert
It's
How things go.

Inarticulate yet speaking

If I drew you
Or me

   As a comic strip character
  Something to read & chuckle
Loudly, Sunday mornings

       You
Or I
       would be
The inarticulate figure
On the bridge, webbed by his own
Sticky contradictions
   Held still, still
      As a cruel moon negotiated
    Gesticulating
Our attempts to speak

  The stage light
If I shifted a theatre rocking horse
For habituation
      Light would spot
The side of face
The cheekbone a sleepwalker
Crashes
  From

     Someone
Maybe
I would be the how of it
    The actor of sorts
& you
You would see.

The vehicle crashed smoking on its side
Gracing some village lawn
  & I'd jump

In my boot cast
		To assist
	Saying
With each my limitations

(She's still moving
I think she's still alive)
	Hearing the dangly earring jangle
But nobody would hear me.

	& when I'd jump in the car again
Silently we'd go forward
Pick
Up
A peanut butter Prairie cookie
	Halving it
	Along our silly way
The webs sticky sticky would fall
In one big sweep
Away

Untitled

Always weird
   This balsa stage of plastic lighting
      Faces peeled
Like cloned masks away.

What ghost follows you, a devoted dog
   Killed then breathed
To life again. Inhabits you

As blood inhabits, feeds. Is fed.
   Ghost father
Waiting hovering over my bad eye
Periphery. Undercover

Ghost dad; always weird. You hiss to me
Of those unholy nights.
      Shrapnel waxing never
Crescent in your flesh

& blood. Plastic eyeball. I guess
I say
      I was that shrapnel too. I bathe from you
That shrapnel too.

For Piper

D 8. 5.22

If there had been a way around it
We'd have chosen that.

But the cactus opened
    The heart cradled like a falcon
Egg in the hand
Bust open.
        A girl & her dog
Left to fend for themselves in a cave.

    Hide n seek
Amidst ice teeth
    White tail deer gathered to salt licks
They lasted for eons.

        But at the end of moonlight
    That columnar shaft
A self philosophers conjure

        Girls grow to women.
& gentle
The most gentle of dogs
Drag their hind quarters
& their constancy falters.

Tired. Too tired.
    The cactus blooms yellow
Bloodletting the hand.

Baby.

Over the peeling sill, OZ

On the sill
A menagerie of bone
   Tree & wish
Whistlers in the August
Dry.

     I cannot see
Over & to the other side.
Stuck stuck
   A remedial absurdity
     Kids driving neon motorcycles
Into trees.

""

Damn.
If I'd only said the thing
To turn everything
   Around

    If only
I'd counted the portents
Off
    These blindsided
Fingers

     Wishbone
   Broke at the fork
Who the long straw
Who the short straw

The
Town square lottery.
It is no fiction.

""

Ah dog days
Ah black dog of Foucault
Depression

The heat was on today.
Her big
Black
Cataract eyes gazing me down.

""

The sill painted red
Peels long in octaves
Like the red Atlantic guitar

Played seaside
The proverbial tide
Damned or
Blessed
Or both. Probably that

To be fair.
Have to stop taking it all on.

""

Addition subtraction

Gentle or swift

The fading in
The fading out

Where, should the
Play write itself, would the spotlight
Shine?

""

Convenience store
Hospital
Tennessee Williams
Laura
That stage set mall light

It shines on nobody
Just a bit to the side
Of a face

Any face
Any face at all

A kind of bird
Elemental beauty.

Whoosh go the deer

sunroom
      blue teal
Armchairs
   We would talk, talk
     light dismissed
Itself & shadows decoded.
      She said
    "when
I loved
I loved fiercely."

""

She said
  (When exile approached
Riding yellow Bedouin horses) —:

"Your daddy
      said stars
are dead light."

          I said " you & I

   Reside   on orchard
Margins & that
Exile is a means toward love. "

Love fiercely.

""

       Once
    light too near
darkness close

She said she was ready
   She carried a glass
Of iced water through lapsing corridors.
   sipped.

They sang.
Left, a blue deer on windfall whoosh.
""

O shrunken skulls on the voodoo wall.
What's your business here?
Cover the cloth with embroidered cloth

All time will stop
        Paused
                    Gently.

Click clack the loom.

Cradles

Grip rag doll
Throw the rag doll
Tear at rag doll hands toes limbs —:

     He spoke. Kiddo
They'd say
Low tones
Amused.

""

      Rubber bands & hook
    Hold plastic dolls
Intact.

       Dolls
Of cloth & down
Are soft as
Pillows

      Easy to suffocate.
    Take the breath
Of the Other
As your own

      His love told him
    Much later
Once the psychiatry
Had ruined

      What faith he'd once
Known. Believing
   Bird
     Tree

Deer & the occasional human
Hitchhiking quietly
Or the

Bicyclist
Nearly smiling

    There was such a secret
Between

        The blue
   Tire
The articulated sweet

    Doll-God
      doll.

Jailbreak

        captive
Padlocked within a purgatory of sorts
    Somewhere between
The first & last knots on the string --:
     Wellness is rarely infinite.

I was afraid.
Always healthy, lucky
  Nerve trees never set afire
That fascist arsonist

A knock on that door
A sliding grip on porch railing
   Breaking bamboo.
Youth I whispered

     But it returned --:
The walking steady.
The fingers deft the opposable thumb.
   No fear of the undertow, dark portent
Of rivers.

Corner

Corner
34th & green mount
Anorexic skyscape
   Men of manifold colors
      Watched

From gated doorways.
  A gentleman, went by Newton,
Handed over
A chocolate almond bar
     Said he knew the tricks
The speed
Of globes, dirt water fire stone or plastic tops spinning festival mantles.

     I gave him my last cigarette
    He ripped the filter
Buttons from a floral dress & kneeling amidst used books on the corner
Of 34th & Greenmount
Rimbaud came to me
His mouth rife with soft yellow Windows
& revelation
   The green globe quickening
      Began.

I saw no vultures

Driving the gentle spiral
Slightly kinked like a barn cat's yellow plumed tail
Birds birds
   cresting up from summer
Holy unholy
  holy feathers nave &
      angular crested
Into the drum of thunder

Drove gently the dusk
  spectral
Imbuing a cumulus humpback
  whale not Quasimodo
A near rainbow crashed through
     Tree hands & leaf
the birds blue
  yellow black
Arrowed through & within a
       language
Inarticulate scrolled a pale
     parchment beyond. Winged.

      Black &
yellow blue.

Untitled

You cuss me out when I cannot find the river
That axial gleam of the North Star
   Molting; now the irrelevant shapeshifter
You cuss me out

      When I find no thread
To tear with my teeth
In that factory.
            Pockets attached to nothing
But the memory
The heat

The heat
   Pressure

A pox you cry
Where has he gone, that boy
Calling forth the astrological retrogrades
      Spinning the fixed stars
Like holiday tops
Spin

            & on some Albany rooftop
      Near Pearl Street
A man nearly boy tells a doubting woman
Love
   Between eras
         Is possible

Even probable
   Lighthouses find shark & mermaid
 At feast together
            Along an eroded shore.

Rewriting desire

Every woman I meet
Called out

I see

     face captive
Hostage of webbed rumor
& insinuation
    I ask each named B
Who sucked color from your yes.
Sucked the timbre from your eyes.

""

Incantations
single
Syllables

 words
   Or just a sultry grunt
Surliness & whiskey
Crested
Crescendo

Blank faced dolls surf
Our streetcars
Trolleys
Users

"

No

   Yes

     cannot be heard
Separate from thin parchment
    Torn mad
       elder skin
Twig harping at portal.

What is congruent
What is incongruity

""

    What happens
When Blanche enters the house of porn.
Nothing more aggravating
    Than to be so sane.

""

What is
The most sacred word.

   Defiance,
      The shadow-wound
Stomped upon by the light the dew of yes.
Chant
Chant

Incantation

""

       Equinox

    Heat
Confronted. Escaped

     Lying on an iron fire escape
   In your underwear. The mosquito.
The bite.

"

Speak out to the ladles, thick with star milk
The Dippers.

Night air is full of everything
Insoluble

Damn hunter's trap

Damn the blessed

The body the physical
World.

Last Drink

Last time I drank the contents
Of a lantern

Scotch was the kerosene
The wick my dancer

A woman wrote of snowmen on fire

It was just another crisis
To leap
    Toward & from

Liberace cut strings of both piano
& harp

My stomach churned chyme milking
      Bulls

What do you do
When everyone around you is devouring lanterns
& learning to remember

How it is
Loving again

Seeing the spirit glimmer
Fireflies the marrow of every rib-tree

The long brief wax
     Museum wick
Of everything.

We

We
        fill drawers with photographs —:
    Or chance upon used bookstore postcards
& young men zipped in trouser
    Tuxedos of discovery
Women slipped in skirts of revelation
Drape bodies across black & white structures
  Perhaps crossroad full of railroad ties
    Or iron wrought bridges
Permit a degree of transparency
  Trouser & skirt blousing with August
Heat & breeze are the other side -- these drawers
Ample grove
      Photos of generations
Men called to battle
  Women to factory. & what are the faces
Of regeneration nuanced pink
    Dear chameleon
      Shapeshifter changeling
Sliding a passage through
  Contradictory worlds.

lemon meringue pie

Someone told you
They glimpse in you both
Clenched knuckle & feather;

    Because you're fragile.

Well aren't you I say
That meringue & lemon melting in the diner
Case; seems I care most
   For the fragile.

Hatchling
Egg shell egg shell

What meets knuckle best? Vagaries
  Sweet

Some fist bump overseas
   Journal

       ribs ground as fact

Spills grit & grain

  When do we condemn
When do we get along

What keeps the future more than a slurred enunciation
    More than

The funeral lily lithograph
That scribing on shadow
    parchment

Yet another idiot
stone by pebble wall.

Deletion

Deletion (the imagined
Conversation)

When I delete a feather
   A word
Poem
Sliver of a photograph
   I compromise
Each response
Each resultant conversation.

""

      Did we ever talk about
The debris
Rubble
Unrest
Essential
   To scribe the brown burnt grasshopper
     Leap
Into image?

""

In Belfast
     Where a woman says
To endure childhood
She got on a bus
Rode end to beginning
Of line
Over & over again.
     From the rubble
  A voice
The firebird rose

      As is often said. Sinéad
Began
Singing out the cobra.

""

Well. The earth is seismic
Virgins cast
Once again
Into the hot orange mouth volcanic
    Perhaps naval
Perhaps umbilical

""

    &, against
A modern anxiety
A paralysis
    You resist
You go to the coop
You feast on figs hands sticky
A necessary transgression

""

  I recall my mother saying
Years back
Of a mother's portrait — there is now
    A child also
In this photograph

A conversation begun
It cannot be deleted
  It cannot be less than a soul

    Captive
  Moving.

""

Here we are
Foreign specks in the eye
  Grit
Grain
Escaping into the space;

Yet another gutted red
    Tusk cage.

For A

A friend

Untitled

A child wakes & by what
Thing is she threaded back to a world
Of matter

  The lamp or lace runner
Or the corner green armchair where the hound rests
Red with dawn. Windows

Parted from sill
    Like mouth of a kid reading orange
  Butterflies into
Existence

Brought to me the August
Whale song the slate colored
    dolphin click click

  & the screams completed
Themselves, tables & chinaware thrown
Articulating

      The civil unrest
    The tripped breakers
  Of a two bedroom home in Pennsylvania

There were no whales nor
Dolphin
     Just a kid waking
  Fingertip fisted to palm

Yet hitchhiker of leaf
Edges light. Light. & necessarily so.

Flamethrower

Flamethrower
Fire eater
    The blue heron in flight
     You state is
A stork. Never seen a stork I say
In the trill of age
Meeting mystery; the repetition source of infancy.
  It returns, the lies, nascent fabrications
     Keeping childhood circumspect, naive.
""

Fire eater
  Wick to the carnival tent. Opens
The flap of camouflage tent like a thin tear of skin.
     Reach high high SO BIG
Daddy would say. High high.
""

    Poetry is only
What it must be. A land mine tripped
  Accidentally
As must be. Ah that berry bled into Lascaux
Caverns
     Bull & horse, sand-dog,
   A motion insatiable
Judy's motorcycle colliding like a stork
The flamethrower potent
    Image
Returned to core of all tree. Birth.
""

   Next bunk bed down
We would hold our breath in each other's hand
Like snow globes full of nightmare lucid
Listen for hooves

In collision. Sandpaper
Rooftops
            Don't tell them what does not exist.
        I found out soon
Enough, harvest
Dribbling from nerves, the smile upturned seized.

A Dare

G said
  I dare you.
Nearly a whisper insidious, Jesus's hiss to sand
Horses; G's hiss
Across that way long wall separating lovers.
     He said: dare
   The tattoo ivy & pitbull & the simulacrum
Of the archetypal red rose
Inking the nape of her neck
       Confronted
    The wall
Disengaged arms of the checkpoint
       & stones crashed
In, graffiti spray painted breast & limb,
The dare
The guess
    Like water begun.

Untitled

The cradle crashed in the sickle moon
Crashed like pheasants up from grass
Laced with blue raven feathers
    & the force of starlings
Inspired to take on a hospital sky. Yellow
Bulldozers trod hills
        As swimmers tread current
River creek time. The hospital
Adolescent alcoholic regeneration
Only an insipid
Chameleon settled
        Into the timbre a unified one.

Untitled

Steamy day sweat tracing spines
Like lullaby hands
   Molting
Lizards of generation

   Crickets drowning slow
In the dry of their own song.

   Told the veterinarians' desk girls
       I don't like people much. Say it
Loud, not confession. We get along
For a greater good
  I say. They laugh. They agree.

I mean
It, true as rain shooting down the bank
  Fog takes from night.
""

      But how to help the one who
Forgets? The one
Dislocated
Hurting
In pain..

   Naming is everything.
     Spell out the days

Into each of his hands, ask what is
Your talisman; from what
   Source, the lantern
By which you gauge the wicked blue
Existence, nickname
     Of your own
Riddler.

Minimum wage

I've done nothing today. But glimpsed
A sailor who looked like me
      Fueling the ship
   Saying that "the albatross "
Is only a monster seagull
Fat & flab of wing.
I was relieved.

      The seagull is pink with
Sunrise
Neon as a strip club sign
Shining
Shining.

         Remembering
  A figure
Grievous grieving
      Set upon by the monster gull
         It still ate souls
Of human
Hope.
         I may bring a minimum wage
      But I can call out defeat
Heat, seizure
& mildly
I am
Mildly amidst locust rattled trees
Relieved.

Morning ale

You speak.
I say I'm tired —:
Too many faces today
Like biology dissection lenses
Smeared
   Toad
Eye of a bull
          When the face is wounded
     A waterfall red blood raft floating

You say
I am worn
Worn as the unicorn
The flailing puppeteer.
             Everyone's fatigue differs
        Too little water drips the IV
The blue butterfly needles
Thin wrist lavender

          Attach the lace of this mirage
To you
That is myself
Mirage to me as well —: six am

     Everyone orders ale.

Untitled

I try to approach with no knowledge.
   Yet full of sky full
Rain
The memory of earth as was
   Before sea —:

I am not tabula rasa.

Today we hit the stores , shopped grapes
   & a bud carnation
      Some items cancel the others
Out
Physically
      Too different, too same

I guess people do that too
An exchange of faces
      Foucault or Rasputin
Insatiable & mad

   Similar or dissimilar

      Who are you
A chant assembled

   futures already complete
In the eyes of leaves & tiger
   Or agate marbles spinning
Cartwheels

      Camelot.
Meh . History. In my damned face again
   Weaker
   More powerful
Taking another round.

Tea Kettles

Someone
   Seated by a cherub pissing fountain
An arc frozen subzero
Said to me
      His face like fog

What is the body but a carcass
Haunted brought back to breath...

         I said what are you
Fog man
      Are you portent
Are you prophecy
Downing constructs of journey
Are you

Holding us back? The earth is strange
As a house
   Skulls found
In the bomb shelter cellar

         Forensics can not pinpoint
   To a human factor

& when the woman calls faint
Disembodied
The kitchen trembles
Fierce
         As our small pink
   Ancient hands.

Gifts

Saw him the other day, the shaman
In peacock headdress.
   I told him a secret.
He was a sketch, the poster,
A whistler on a wall.
The night before
He cut a wedge into my breast.
(It's how one deveins a trout, I hear him
      Politely say) I saw a doe
Victorious
On a back road
A clearing of dancers.

   They put the jar
With a pink wedge of me
On a shelf somewhere
(Not cancer
The shaman said
   Like a hen wishing bone on a sill.)

I saw these people
Deer
     Arrowheads significant in a blue shot glass
I saw
   On a barroom breakfast table
Beside a newspaper & a glass of grapefruit juice.
& the shaman
Gifted because crippled
     Seeming you.
   & you waited
Like a raven biding the temperament of skies.
  The departure of exile. Skies.

Voting dusk

Walking home
  Wishing a transistor radio shook song
About wonder
Sight
    Rain
In the back pocket of my jeans:
But that's long ago now.
        Kids catcall from the trail
Closed at dusk. Call me
Hey You
Hey Lady
      Hey!
          I duck the street lamp rampant
    Look as I meander
In wide open mouths
Full of brass candles
Parrots
    & pianos or the occasional room dark
As a bedroom closet.
Closed doors --
        Stranger
In Algiers no just upstate but who knows who
Is a sieve of impulsivity
With or without a weapon. Truly.
      Sensual August
Carries me to the other wall of heat.
I push the paper
To the lips of the dark machine.
    Push the door against
          Humidity, tomorrow .

Skyscrapers

Guessing when the air broke
Like skylights beneath you
   You decided to dump
Your boa & good for nothing wings

& guessing
When the wizard said he wished
   He had a wand, his tool
Was bent & torn

       You knew
For sure

There are people hitching
Or giving rides
      Who you
Mistrusted & could not love
As you were told

To
Love. Repercussions yes. But you
Are not Plath's kin & confessors exhaust
   As
Much as do confessions. So shhh
      Your mouth girl.
Shut your mouth.

The sky is blue.
That's all that they want or need
   To know.

GRIEF

(We put a letter in a blue & white post
Box pickup noon.)

  remember
      the folding

Paper airplanes sacred as origami hounds
   & blue nosed pits

How we'd shove the scythed
      wings a bit
Against the current

   & it would push
Into the other side of gravity's
      rage
Sometimes even
Levitating

   Lazarus
Or the magician's assistant —: what is
Beauty, invisibility

Whichever arrived to the winking red
      rail tie
Crossroads first /

     Or the guardrail
Crashed in.

To Raymond

    Early on
At 9
Even
  trees became
Unreliable. As self
Exiles self
I asked the sketch pad
What is friend

""

        When you drive Brookside
By the Hudson
        low Catskills
Advance to you like winter
Salt licks where congregate

Deer of March fertility &
    There is
That argument with witness
Engaged
    Electrocardiography
    Shadow haunt
        & surveillance paranormal

You realize
There is a hex cast
& love is strange

""

I still ask
        Eyes painted eyes follow
            From that portrait on the mantle
    Sly those eyes
Sly

""

137

   & Ray
I hear you say
" how dare you judge
Me"
" I dared to love
You
   Despite/because "

""

Truly
It's nothing revolutionary
This version of the self
Hungry

Running toward
Running away.

""

There's a song about it
  Shamed

How I stand still
  At the sill of becoming

& you are a zillion miles away

Are you still angry
  Ray

""

  This dark house
Guest
   feeds

On fear & unacknowledged
  Trials
      Bright green eyed tigers
Must be confronted
For the planks
& cellar to settle.

""

How dare you judge me he said.
How dare I judge you I say.

The monster now

In the middle of sipping
        saccharine
Poison at the dim lit bar
  I let a purple Mickey Mouse blotter
Melt on
    My candor. We watched
Romeo bare-assed on a movie screen.

  Juliet expired innocuously like a cardboard milk carton
      Date
Or the birth tattooed on a racing greyhound's inner ear
  flap &

You lunged
Midst grope
  Claimed

I looked like someone almost familiar.

You will never think you're worthy
     You uttered:

I said well Sam said we are all
Just climbing out
Of a dusky kitchen trash can.
X & x. Or generational

Customs. "Shame on you."
The DNA coiling like a toy Slinky
  Touched
Like a dark spirit
&, feeling the saxophone tremble
I left. Emptiness

Hung in the air
A monster's perfume &
  My boots clicked

Like an exorcised porpoise —:
Who is the monster now.

Hauled

Sometimes I forget
It's less about being forsaken
As it was about
   Forsaking. Wilderness in your violet
Hair , kiddo, why I didn't see death as home; didn't salute
      The advent calendar
Doors shuffling open
In the surgery walls. Those muted calls.

I guess they hauled me like a fallen
Calvary horse
Into front loader —: like a house
Eave where crow feathers
   Settle in the dew
Signifying life
Though in groups of three they mean
Guardian
      Or devastation..

It doesn't matter

It doesn't matter I say
It doesn't matter
   Levitating
  Somewhere between infirm & well —
If we remember the same
Events
   As unfortunate
     The instant the assault
Began. What is safety? Teddy bear
Teddy bear.
    Wind spoons your body when you
Screw things up simply by breathing
  You are left on the highway. God fury
& his return. But we ate gladly
Popsicles too & raced them amongst
     Rivulet & grain of rain
Water & laughed or ran silent
Taut in our own ribs of
Existing
    Of exacting self discipline
From paths of sugar water winding
The rings
    Trees bear
       Like weddings.

A night in Albany

A night in Albany
   By a field of picnic tables

Bicyclists everywhere
A grid a crosshatch
  So many colors —; that's the yellow
     Wheel
    Tripped over in that junkyard
    Busting through a sculptor's roof
Germany

So weird
Bicycles the oiled chain
Upon which even wind depends
  Long ago stranded on a highway
Once back road
     I dialed my second most physical lover
From a blue tooth booth
Pay phone.

He had a thing
About disappearing through
Windows; a thing about
  Taking glue trapped mice
  & helping them break
As from an electric chair
     That person strapped down

Like a woman
Falsely accused. Who breaks out
   Of the sculptor's rooftop
  A curl
A train
     Transgressions
    The way to everyone
Bicycling by a statue

Moses wrought. Maybe
A sea undead.

The tattoo artists arrive

The tattoo artists arrive
   in 27 minutes.

Men in purple —: no white jacket surely
  Wrapped round & round
Stone river bends.

Bracelet ?
To adorn / cover
The body a volcano of immolation
  Wounds are flowers
Perhaps black orchids
    Or festival lilies
Anyway
As detritus is washed
   & claimed by another
World. I see a hound's golden face
Settled amongst
Folded cuffs combat boots
  I see the blue
Iris
  She brought in yellow boxes
    Unfurled & planted in
That garden
With
Just a smudge of protective sage.
Skin Walker.
Stay clear.
     Bracelets dominance
Cuff disguise.
   I am well now. Today
This minute
Maybe at midnight.

    I love you, the ones
  Who have stood at the

Bus stop
In the rain for me
    Where is the black
Umbrella. In the dusty corner
  I will bring it to you
Crashing mirrors
Believing in luck.
    The fortune teller tossed rainbow
          scarves
At our feet
She clicks the language of underground seas.
Sometimes
    In the raw meat of moon
I believe her.

Reading Hesse

I saw
I was mired
In a house of horror

    Dogs trembled at the clasps
Of fire

   Someone went
Into my drawers & betrayed
What I wanted

To become.
   In one gargantuan mirror someone
With my face
Body
Hands

      Killed somebody.

Philip used to say

We are all capable of murder

   As he grunted
Nietzsche

Doggy style

& made even
The looking glass bleed.

Untitled

He looked away to catch
His breath; amused

     she realized
It was not because
she was
    lovely. She was
just dilapidated
Infirm
Somehow
    round
Faced a bit
Unnerving

Where is my hat
She cried
Where
Is my boa
Draped
Over my oxen
Stake
The stuff
That instincts are made of? He turned

To her.
Here
Is
Your hat
He said
& handed
Her a
Pub cap
    Green
The light feather edges
Of a leaf

Cutting
But only a little.

Watermarks

Yea
            water evaporates
Recedes
"Goes elsewhere—"

I see the shells
    Ground down
Or fossil watermarks of that which
Some say are
            Pterodactyl wings.
The same ledge as
A human
Footprint

"Were you there"

        Stamped on the kitchen walls
Above kitchen towels

""

    truth be
I inhabited
The chair twice:

Electric

            Salvation

        I was 16, seeing climbers
Crawl the nape of peaks
    & when light gashed horizon
Like a lamb's squeak
I forgave myself. But only for a moment.

    Secondly
Having divorced deity
Loudly
    A landslide
Got me

My kid's Sunday school pigtails

Being
So much pain
My pelvis levitated. I saw

I was unfortunately
Seen a woman face & body pulse so
Common

Ordinary

   What is invisibility if not
The purest intent.

""

    My mother
Only said
damn yet
      I was making amends of sorts
    To the shell of her
Weeping. I listened
   & I was told

Hell is on earth; of
Our own making

Cockroaches scurrying along
The scape of things

The damned scarecrows

""

    That's what stays

When someone says
This is what
I think
What do you
Think

In some dialogue of
Truth &
Joy

Dammit

""

     I see you naming fossils
        Down in the quarry
Pennsylvania

Kids
We swam anyway
Despite many projections
That all children drowned
    Eventually

By whatever means
Watermelon of
    justice

Swallowed or spent
unwanted violent white spray
    Spermatozoa
Scrubbed

Trucker
From the hipbone.

Transparency

From the ice-cube
Transparent of the invariable
Shit we venture into the other,
Clock-in click-out
Via the factory card.

We've been meaning to paint
Over this lucid dream; binocular
Ventures of ice queen & griffin.

You often correct me --:
Before waiters servants & gods
They who slip raw espionage hands into coven
Drawers man this is only
The wall of child scribbles --:

Of plastic cerulean stars kettle-spouted
Glued to a ceiling
Stucco of a deer hunter signature. Idiot me.

Yes booked ink fingerprint .
I tell you
I've never loved enough
& my dear you were angry
For you wanted to love for all of time.

The blue kettle transports us home
Where air doesn't stink
      These paper
Mills
Driving the damned water.

I've written about iguanas

          having never met
     An iguana outside
The terrarium & black strobe light
Or heat lamp? -- that elephantine skin, wrinkles
Momentary, belong to orphaned
Beings stranded in drives
Inhuman.

      So
In my benign interpretation
   I am seeing elephants where once
      Rested Catherine's pet
Iguana
               Or memory of leaning over
   Some piano
Witness gutted into a draftsman table.
Crying
Having flown to San Francisco
Too drunk to love
Rife
      Cloud banks vaguely disclosing that tree
            Too drunk, for touch
Rejected, sex of him flaunted & fast
To someone else
In the next room
               & all you do then
      Is cry into shining towers of crippled narcissus
Or Formica
Tiles on the counter:
Aware; sometimes friends
Thousands of miles away
      Counter us
            Lose us
      Hear the mother animal wail, might be

An elephants pierce
A loving grief // grief, of love.

Memory of driven taxis

Drove a cab lasted a day or so
Trainer said I wouldn't make it. Cut
Moon big as a Vegas token
Whatever desert gamblers use
When the ring grows into
Flesh when skin sheer as glass
Loops around the diamond
Strange truth & falsehood
Seem apparent here.

""

But you watch bedrooms
With your Audubon binoculars
What bird you're seeking
I've no idea
    but Stewart
Always knew what the moon
Was at essence
The slurp water makes slushing the iron door
Between sleeping babies
& the seismic
Song schoolbooks mounded
In gentle thuds

This is only the memory
Of that tsunami
Swooshed yellow cabs off bridges
Just as ships
Of espionage were coming through
O Nagasaki
How many gardens
For so many wounds.

""

Just weird
How we see things differently
Even from the same telescope
Book of astronomy
Binoculars belonging to that man

A palsied hand
A bird feeder red & brass.
Must cut that oak
To fit a feeder in that fenced yard
We approach facts
& somehow
The endgame corrupts
As too it is
Corrupted

""

Old man
Dyed yellow
Your hail is a signifier
You say you're a hawk
You say you're noble
But someone whispers
Hitler looked up to Zarathustra
As he patted down his horses
After his daily
Single meal

What, a slab of bull
What, that thick cream clogging
Whatever space remains
Between disbelief & fear
Someone somewhere sings
Of Rushdie stabbed
Eye lost
As blindness exists
Especially in heaven

Captive Orchards

Not that strange. Epiphanies
Are a hand captive
In a sun shaft that
As it appears
So it swiftly goes. A squirrel
Dodging the wheel
  Of course
     Even when in exile
  You kiss partners
Through bullheadedness
That bubble wrap popping
As dogs dance
& dancing

     Well. I put
Him in exile, birthday cards already
Written
Another daughter's signature
Only vaguely similar
To my own.

    Strange. How sometimes
  Love is intangible
Too subtle. Hands flash
    Edges like spent leaves
Unfurling

Like little blue fags
Made of paperback history
Books, the kind of history
  That is easily
    Piled
& burned. &
  Is it love, then?
     Who can tell, hitch-hiker.

Whistling Moons

I know the moon
Is composed mostly of whistles.
   I have seen it
Heard it
Felt
It

     Ebb & flow where the noise
Was growing exponentially.
        Meaning didn't matter.

  Sailors at port
Teach delinquent kids
To lay down cigarette or machete
     Gather up blades of onion grass
To purse to whistle upon.

I have seen sickle dark moons
Turn my kid's smile
    Upside down & leave aliens closer
To home
Than are the homeward bound.

Cluck the tongue
As the goose
Gathers her brood
   & whistling
Bring the moon home; no grave

Victorian age portrait but just the moon
  Rife with children
Sailors
Unpopular referees.

Chesapeake Bay

August
Becket looming
   "Make your own tapestry"
   The fuel stink the engine
Falling away

      Round
   Orb of a face

Slit green eyes
  The androgyne
Water so shiny it might kill
Anything you once
Believed.

      By the harbor
   The yellow rowboat rocked
& cadence of froth current against
The unnecessary
Rudder

     Changed the sloppy meticulous
Tide to a Seuss
Character indeed a slim bound story.
& my love

   That's the way

It was. Feathers were not fists at all
   & hunger was temporary
Release from flesh a kind of
      Muted catcall.

the zoo is prodigal

We see them go
   The beauty mammalian // not quite
      Elephant or dolphin
But almost a slate
   Grey. In old black & white film
      Grey (a graduated hue) meant red

The black widow hourglass
   A shade of hair
       A bowler cap usually black
Revolutionized.
   Where is the median asks the student
      Struck down: just as
Some force elliptical
   Machine tossed him high.
        Never came across a kid in coma
     But your heart
Stopped
   You lost a few moments of
      Most essential air. What happens after that
Never matters. Not really. Only that you managed to exhale
   & inhale again. Jaws clatter
     We inhaled too.

Dogs know

All knowing these
      Red & gold bloodhounds gentle
  Ears draped over their cheeks
Baying in hide n seek
Countdown.

    I once had such a dog
Ben his name
Whose burial I was denied
At foreboding of red fox & village
Coyote darting amidst
Copses of oak

     His skull was a tepee
  Indented
From Lyme yet
Gifted as the omniscient shaman
  He would open the humongous
      refrigerator
   & dip his paw
Into plates of sweet potato pie.

Kilns

nearly ceramic
A grey vase hollowed
By potter's hands the wheel spinning
But like angel glass
Deadly to the hungry
She was cast to walls, cast herself.

    Damn heat of kiln.
  She spoke bright
Bright as memory of having memories
As seagulls recalling tourist French fries
    & flight steady
        Permeating layered clouds

Sunsets
Peeking mauve as bled-out umbilicus
Found knotted
Full of mortality on white bright nervous sands.

Untitled

Lazing about the voluptuous landscape
Moon near as
    The nuclear
Plant
      3 towers peaking
The Susquehanna. We won't go kayaking this year
I say -- end of summer
Has arrived
Some trees already touched by
Scarlet. But damn this emerald
    Soft moss beneath us
Our spines press their spooned vertebrae
& we make our mark
    As waters go in coming years
This moment will be somebody's prehistory
A boy will range the bed &
    Discover
The bright fossils of our
    wings. This kiss
The muscle of it
    Will go on,
        Carry on.

Road kills & night smoke

Gaze
    steadfast, lighthouse
Grounded in stone cliff
  Child, mine.
      Green eyes, blue.
Could've gauged it differently
I guess.
       no exit
Signs
Winked from wall
Space age corridor
    being
      the firm
Covenant it is. Yet
A drifting in & out, swimming
A crab's scuttle
  There was
    Truly no entry as no
Iron red fire escape, it was //
It is what it is.
    I repeated
Repetitions of heritage
  That grassy dune at night,
The knoll
Anonymous
Orchards pink & hallowed
    & pirates come to shore
  Earrings
Tearing flesh, lobe
The meat of it
    Moon gnawed down by hut, by castle
As I sought to teach
The o so
    stubborn one

There are easy ways to say it.

Syllables
Round
Unbreakable.
    Crushed against the glass
Holding ice water
An ant
A grasshopper

A woodpecker ramming.
       Easier ways, than this speech
Of clouds scissored
Into many pieces; a photograph
Panic covets. Destroys.

    Destroyer
Hannibal, Banes
Masks like world globes hollowed
& slipped over
The head
      A pirate's patch.
I send you a throw sturdy continents sprawling...
        an endless
   Silence. An endless sea
Contours everything.

Pink

There's been lots of talk
About the end of the world.

The bee that stopped settling
    Upon the ripe flower. Yet napping
  In the masochistic noon light

I've seen the brink
That's difficult to reach — &
  Not reaching
      Determines everything —:

Old men hum with hands looping
The dancer's waist. Pink

   transparent dragonfly
Skimming the Harpeth Knoll
River

      Leaves contrail
Magnificent
As the pink spacecraft wake

    Piercing
The atmosphere &

        maybe it's
Ok to consider
  In terms of
Neither finish nor begin

    Just the long inhale
  Floating // we are softly

Bobbing
  a lake buoy
swimming
  In morning rain.

By the water

We ordered dense Germanic coffees
  Some
        Yellow haired woman kept calling you
By many names.

The dented suitcase
Of stapled red leather trembled; I carry my voices
In there you said.

  Sometimes there is nothing
To be done; some people leave me piled
Like graffiti bricks red
Cinder

        Smoking
Rockets of independence days. Nothing.
So you say
                I know it has nothing to do
With me. I know
You said

            We will never pause
      Hip to hip
Point to gash & flower

As they say, you said. Some people hover
Just beyond
That resistance parachute torn, hung black
In the tree line
Just past that painter's house. I knew him well
      I said.
                He taught me the texture
The crosshatch graphite
Of boats
I said: a kid on a charcoal bridge
Smudged

& vaguely
Like daffodil remnants
disturbed.

VOICE

this village slept, our dogs
Heard the shriek, coyote or cat, fox
& let loose. Bay, singing,
Bay. Lights sprang open.

""

I see
    Her dog beautiful
without bark,
noiseless. think Chinese kiosks,,
Streetside, snap voice box strands,
Snap, cello strings.

Voice, objectified.

""

        Silence creaks
Scatters attic bats against eaves
Hollow trapdoors, skylight
Where zen endorses sky scape
Of suffering — going on
Like kids standing like lost heron
On ice webbed, webs spreading
Around the slight weight,
    Blue cracking,
Giving in.

Isosceles triangles amidst the branches.

Quarry.
Has an agent tried to destroy
You, reach back
Into the yawning throat of
Compass, values —:
Yanking forth

What we sing,
Big Bangs,
  Orange spark prescient
To the thing creeping
Tagging the fence,
The blue door.

TOWER OF HOLLOWS

There are cliffs then there are cliffs.
Some sand, some stone. Some lined with transient slate blue linens
A fencing the wind will prove ephemeral.
   That's what that debris is,
Moved with a yellow crane; upon which stands,
Erect as a ginger-cat tower,
A blue heron.
Its beauty can capsize a canoe.

Ah, erasure. Not only the lipstick smear,
The smudge of violet eye shadow.
Not only my very Celtic genetics, the dangly
   Letters of my final name.

I would not have told you any of it.
Passing through, I haven't the wisdom of Zarathustra
I haven't the patience of a termite,
   Burrowing to form a tower of hollows.
I'm just some woman, maybe a lady, maybe
A katydid, watching from the margins, an outsider
Smearing the binocular lens that all might be
Trusted, impossibly, to be

      Refuge,
Integral,
Safe & nearly neutral,
      With the beauty of the Great Pyramids,
Of wonder mostly because
They are no graveyard, exist
Levitational, gravitational,
Without purpose but for the play / light
   With shadow, form cast
In sundown dissolved, of sudden
Dissolves.

BEEN HERE 2 DAYS

Left the house two days ago
  Came back
Clutched crisscross guru
Branches
     red plums fleshed
  Flashed
An imaginary yellow yet the painted
    Awning of this unbroken house.

I heard the bark
    of a broken wolf
Hover in clouds
  With stars.
      She spoke as to a lifelong mate.

Two days I've survived inside
Eating grapes withered
  Red boxed raisins
Scratching mirrors
     With angels of fear
  Dissolving distances
what takes me in & breathes me out.

     Foothills dappled snow
  & cape-draped horses.
& the memory of rage
As you clutched me near
In your trembling age.

I'm behind a wall of pain. Origami
  Swans
    Circling the milk
& the view from here
     breath taking //
  seldom understood. Dead house

No, dead house no.

INNER LIMITS

We aren't finished. Space opens
Like a taxi door the yawn of a yellow
Tulip. I'm not waiting for summer /
Pomegranate return. Winter light
Passes through my body-:

      pores are sky lit

Portals. My friend climbs icebergs
Seeking plants & mollusks in pockets
Of air & when he returns we wait for
Hot pekoe tea & I do not ask: What
or who have you left roadside, babe.

Oil Rainbows

It's not the future that scares me
It's history sneaking
    Treading light as a dragonfly pink
  Skims the surface
Of rivers.

We once played monsters—:
Dove into the underwater darknesses
      Dodged shafted summer orange
    Light as storm metamorphosed
In a moment

All the ugliness the young
Fathom — into rainbow. Spectral
        Arc children confront
   Oil puddling, marking the space
Where love, rib chassis bone, parked.

      What happened the night before
   Was there desperation back rub
A cat or table or cast iron
Tea kettle
    Whistling contrails as they flew

A kind of vanishing only children remember
     Like the ability to see through
   Ribcage canary
Into the sixth sense stuck heart
Dead.

OF ABANDON:

Consequence Wit Nonsense

     Witty
  The wit of time knitting night with
Day
    By moon-knot rising
Falling
Oblique giving way.

Last night he ran about the mansion
Two rooms a refrigerator
Nearly a bathroom
    Screaming
       Without a dip into the consequence
Nonsense grants:

Why does everything go
Away
       Everyone

& to the zigzag light of a dog yard
The shit of snow/thaw
Appearing
      (rake some rabbit hay she says
  A nagging background
Inflection)

      A lozenge
Dissolves into the bleak of it.
& he crouches
  Like a humanity hunted
      Down, down.